Morteza

Morteza

Poems by

Neil Creighton

Cover design by Shay Culligan
Cover photo by James E. Lewis

ISBN: 978-1-63980-074-2

Kelsay Books
502 South 1040 East, A-119
American Fork, Utah 84003
Kelsaybooks.com

For all refugees and victims of war

Author’s Note

These poems are a work of fiction. The three characters, Morteza, Rosa and Atefeh, are fictional. Whilst some parts of Morteza’s story parallel the experiences of refugee and surgeon, Munjed Al Muderis, these poems are in no way intended as a biography. Munjed Al Muderis is an inspiring real life person but any parallels are used only as a starting point for the poems’ wider themes.

Acknowledgments

Guy Farmer's Social Justice Poetry: "Nightmare"

New Verse News: "On Massacres in Schools" (first published as "Cost")

One Sentence Poetry: "the spider's silken geometry" "A Beam of Light"

Praxis Mag Online: "Morteza Meditates" (Published as "I Am, We Are"); "The Forge"

Rat's Ass Review: "fog" "At the Hustings"

Verse-Virtual: "Morteza's Escape" "Choice" "Hold Me" "Final Night" "On the High Roof Top" "A New King" "Dispersion" "On War" (first published as "Metastasis")

Contents

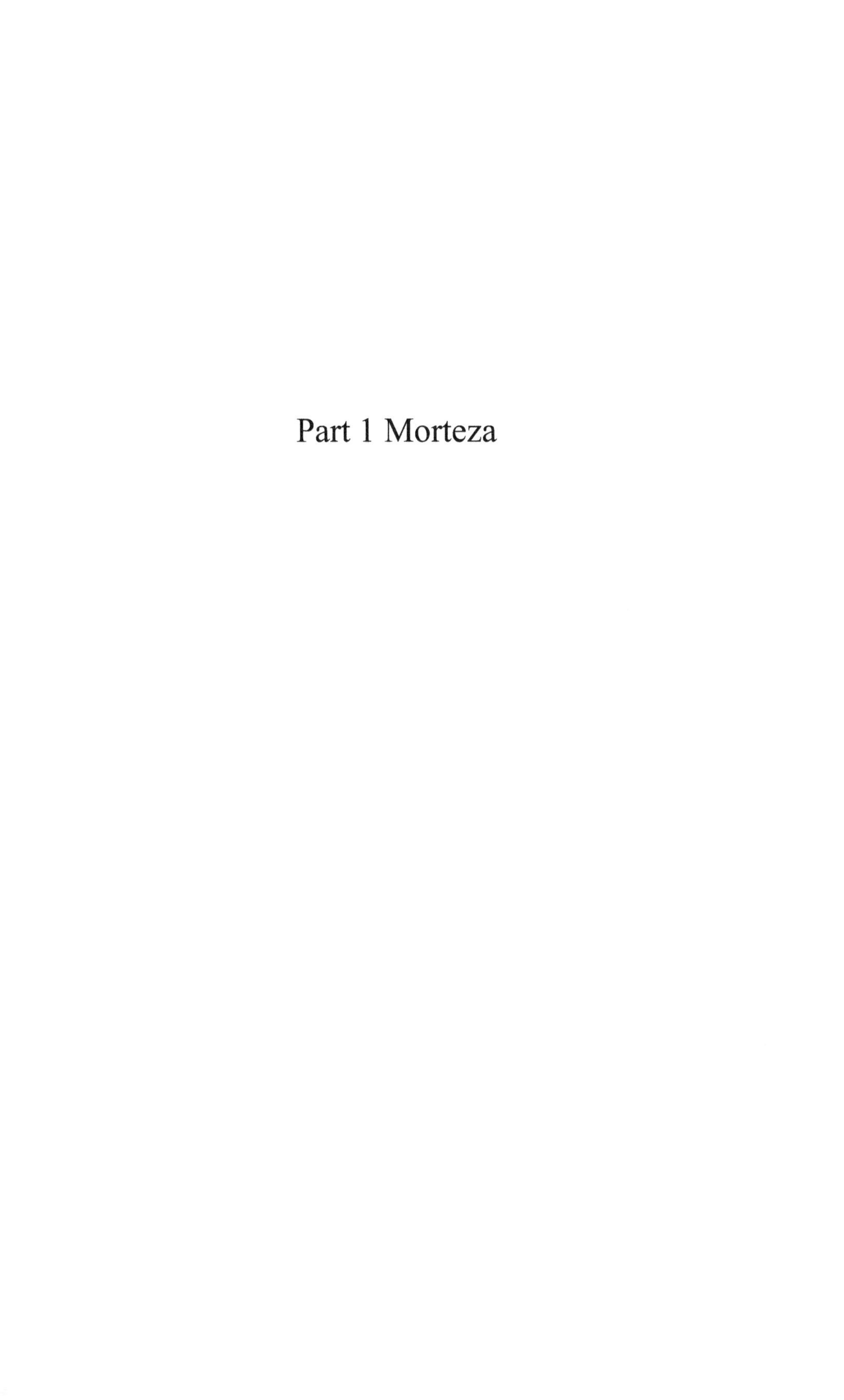

Part 1 Morteza

Morteza's Escape

Strange how memory is triggered.
Strange how sight, sound or especially smell
can bring a sudden rush of recollection.
That is what happened to Morteza
as he walked along the hospital corridor.
Instant flashback.
He was thirty years into the past.
He sees again his professor
being marched from the hospital.
He hears the staccato burst of gunfire.
He knows he will be next.
He hides for hours in the women's toilet.
He rushes home, gathers what he can,
kisses his parents, cries, hugs them,
and then his brother is driving him
through the city's shadows
and up into the high mountains,
both praying that there will be
no unknown checkpoint.
They know of a snow-filled pass,
a dangerous route with no road
but one that avoids the guarded border crossing.
He hugs his brother.
They weep.
Two tribesmen wait.
He has paid them well.
He mounts a sturdy little pony
and for three days they lead him
through the mountains,
one high white peak replacing another.
He is numb beyond exhaustion.
Sometimes his horse sinks to its chest.
He dismounts and struggling,

labors through deep snow drifts.
Then, there is the last peak
and a long way below, like a patchwork quilt,
the panorama of the plain,
a sprawling refugee camp,
heat and hopelessness,
more travelling days filled with fear,
people smugglers charging exorbitantly,
a dangerous journey by sea
in a crowded little boat that crests and drops
for hundreds of kilometers on the open ocean
until finally, an island,
part of the wealthy empire that he believes
values freedom and individual rights
but which he will much later call “Babylon”.
A wave of relief sweeps over him.
He makes his plea for asylum.

Uniformed people take him a long way.
The blazing sun batters
a collection of crude huts huddling
in unending desert flatness.
The sky is uninterrupted blue.
The low scrub is grey/green,
the earth an ochre red.
Razor wire tops high fences.
Guards are contemptuous and callous.
A number is scrawled on his shoulder.
He is thrown into solitary confinement.
Still he studies, despite the deprivations.
He will not waste this time.
He waits for almost a year.
His plea is successful.

It is a ticket to freedom, to life, to love, to children,
to the exercising of his extraordinary gifts,
to a life of service, to mending broken bodies.

He knows he was lucky.
Some years later gates were closed,
families were separated
and asylum seekers were sent
to a bleak, barren, treeless island
in the middle of the trackless sea.
There they stayed, year after year,
abused, despised by the locals,
shrinking little by little,
their gifts unrecognized and unused.
What would he have done?
Would he, in bitterness and despair,
have chosen the option of some others?
Would anyone have wept for him?
Who would have mourned him?
Who would have remembered him?

He shakes his head and chastises himself.
This full day cannot permit indulgence.
Too many need his help.
The present must take all his attention.
As he walks down the corridor
he can see limbless crowds waiting.

Morteza's Choice

The river beneath the ancient bridge
ran wide, fast and full,
surging, eddying, swirling
but channeled, compelled, choiceless.
Above it a hawk circled.
Somewhere, he thought, *a mouse*
trembles beneath a taloned shadow.
Somewhere, necessity drives the lion to kill.
Somewhere, the fleet deer leaps.
And I have once more returned
to the place of my birth.

He remembers that occasion of his first return,
how a wave of fear swept over him,
unnerving him when he saw at the airport
a posse of armed soldiers
and the mustachioed general standing beside
the cold-eyed, unsmiling cleric.
They were his welcoming committee.
He was certain they knew his background.
Long ago he had fled as a refugee
but he was returning as a celebrity,
the great surgeon and philanthropist
from the other side of the world.
He looked down and floating in the river
was a vision of long lines of amputees,
a tidal flow of faces filled desolation and hope.
They had come to him as their miracle worker.
He sees the battlefield,
twisted and burnt vehicles
and lastly, the marketplace,
its ruined and teetering buildings,
the smoke, stench, blood, litter,
groans, screaming and death.

Is everything the blindness of chance,
random, time and circumstance converging
to deal out fate or fortune?
Young people walked innocently along
at the precise moment when a truck
packed with death exploded
and took their legs or their life.

The vision fades. In the flooding river
are little islands of logs, branches and refuse
caught in irresistible surge.

The storm must break.
The hawk must circle and stoop.
The lion will lie waiting downwind,
and I have returned to my birthplace,
not because I am caught in currents
more powerful than my will
but because it is my choice.
That is my power and my privilege.
Others more noble have gone before.
Many better are still to follow.

Atefeh

She had lost both legs above the knee.
Government would not help her.
She could never afford prosthetics,
not the kind he was offering.
Meeting her, he was amazed
by her spirit, her resolve, her refusal
to be bowed by adversity,
her fierce humor and her indomitable will.
Morteza could not wipe her image from his mind.
He met with her for some days and talked to her.
Mostly, he asked her questions
and awe struck, listened to her replies.
His time was limited.
The prosthetics were expensive.
He must choose carefully.
Finally, he made up his mind.

I will help you, he said.
I will make you walk again.
Many in my adopted country
are kind and generous.
We will raise money for you.
I will return next year.
Then I will give you legs.

She did not speak.
For a moment she sat there, looking at him.
She took his hand and kissed it.
She had no place for tears.
They could not exist in her world.
She nodded, called for her mother, and left.
He could see how deeply moved she was.
He ached, not just for her,
but for all the needless suffering of the world.

Hold Me

He lay on his bed.
He was mentally exhausted.
He had lost his fine balance
between the steel of resolve
and the softness of compassion.
He wanted to weep.
He longed for his wife.
If only he could hold her.
The world seemed so mingle-mixed,
so disproportionately fixed,
sometimes tenderly molded
but too often savagely, cruelly hewn.
Please, he thought, *come to me.*
I know you are on the other side of the world.
It is morning and you are working
but I need you, now.
Reach out for me, somehow.
Bathe me in your wonder and light.
Grant me your sweet respite.
Please, wash away this night.

Final Night

Sleep fled.
Useless to try.
His work was finished.
Tomorrow he was going home.
Despite his exhaustion,
he felt a strange sense of peace.
He climbed to the roof of his hotel.
Far away, on the other side of the world,
his city of glittering glass towers
neon-blazed all through the night,
but night wrapped in silence and darkness
this low slung city of ancient buildings.
No late night revelers shouted and laughed.
The Guard had put an end to that.
Their brutal, egotistical emptiness
flicked only momentarily through his mind.
This was not a night for sadness.
He had done what he could,
brought healing to some
and accepted what he could not change.
He looked over the city and then upwards.
The sky blazed with light,
the Milky Way a white swathe.
He felt connected to everything,
the stars, the sky,
the people he imagined
lying quietly in their beds.
Were they not his brothers and sisters?
Were they not all one?

Morteza Meditates

I am the wind that ripples the water,
the sun rising from the sea,
the dark clouds scudding the sky,
the leaf that falls from the tree,
the womb in which I was woven,
ten million million words that whirl,
my love who shares my body and mind,
the little child's hand enclosed by mine.

I cannot lift my hand against you, my brother,
abuse or oppress you, my sister,
exploit you, my neighbor,
or burden you, my little ones.
We are all the wind that ripples the water,
the curling swell upon the sea,
the clouds that billow, wisp or scud,
the momentary glory in the west
the darkening mystery of the night.

Part 2 Morteza's Diary

Return

Morteza should have been deeply content. He was home in his lovely apartment high above the city. Rosa was sleeping quietly beside him. Yet he couldn't sleep. He was so disturbed by what had happened when he arrived at the airport. He had expected the same dull routine that had happened every other time. This time, however, was different.

The customs officer had looked at him suspiciously, asked him from where he was returning, made a phone call, told him to wait. Then several uniformed officers arrived, led him away to a small room and began asking him questions. Where was he born? Where had he been? What was his business there? What was his religion? How often did he return? Who did he know there?

He told them he was a surgeon. He had been a citizen in this country for thirty years. What business did they have with his religion? He came to this country as a refugee. Every year he led a medical team to the country of his birth. There was a great deal he could do there. Thousands had lost their limbs. He gave them prosthetics, first attaching titanium rods to their bones and the prosthetics to the rods. Others in his team were anesthetists, physiotherapists and nurses. He had been away a month and now he was home.

Later, he said to Rosa: "They treated me with contempt. They looked at me as if I was an enemy. They questioned me. Then left me for a long time. Then they came back and said I could go. They still looked at me with disdain, as if I was something contemptible. I don't understand. Why is this happening?"

"There is a new government," Rosa said. "It's all very ugly. A great deal of hatred has been let loose. There is a ban on all people from our old country. It is that old story. Find scapegoats and blame them for everything. Your face reveals your origin. They think everyone from our country is a terrorist. We are all under suspicion."

In the dark, Morteza thought about the last thirty years. He had been overwhelmed with joy at the liberty he had found, at the opportunities his new country had provided, at the wealth and honor it had conferred upon him. He was not so foolish as to think everything was perfect. He knew its history, the struggles of its past, the deep racism in some areas, its wars with itself, its paradoxes, the Bible in one hand and the gun in the other, its extremes of wealth and poverty, the smoldering divisions of politics, race and wealth.

Yet he had believed in its ideals, its sense of government, freedom and opportunity. Were these all threatened? Were they so tenuous that a new government and a maliciously narcissistic leader could sweep them away?

He lay for a long time. Finally, he arose, went to his desk, took out his most precious diary, the one he kept for his most private thoughts, and began to write.

Increasingly disturbed, he would continue to periodically write until he again returned to the war damaged country of his birth.

fog

descends
thick
impenetrable

hiding
mountain
trees
paths
the poor
the dispossessed

and I grope
despair
long for light

imagine
the clarity
of the sun

yearn
for a glimpse
of the distant
mountain's
foothills

ache
for a low slung
single star
shining white
beside
a sliver moon.

A New King

The axis of my world has shifted.
Old verities chaotically fly
into fog incomprehensibly blank.
Has gravity lost power to hold?
Can eyes no longer discern direction?
The new king is a charlatan
beating at the hollow chest
of his own vast emptiness,
a low grade thief who stuffs
the crown jewels into his pocket,
then peacock-struts, flaunting
them in pride of ownership.

I fled oppression.
This city gave me freedom,
conferred on me honor and wealth,
enabled me to help others,
gave me hope for the future
and belief in the rule of law.
I cannot sleep.
I fear the blank emptiness of fog
winding through the streets,
covering the city, blanketing
even the unseen landscape
that stretches ominously
beyond the confines of this city.

On the High Roof Top

Fog covers Babylon.
Fog covers walls, river,
palaces, canyons of glass.
I take the lift to the roof.
I look out into the whiteness.
I know the roads are choked with refugees.
I know too that it is hope
that buoys them, makes them risk all
in dangerous seas, foreign lands,
makes them calculate the danger
of pirates, criminals and murderous smugglers
for the dream of freedom in the golden city.

This city is my home.
Once it was so generous of spirit.
It opened its doors to the needy.
Now its mighty gates are locked and barred.
Its heart is hardened.
Detention centers darkly flower
on barren islands far away.
Children are torn from their parents.
Everywhere I hear angry shouts of hate.
Mobs roam the streets.
How has her heart become so dark?
Bright lights drew me to the golden city.
Have they forever dimmed?

The Best That We Can Do?

The only sound was the flat slap
of waves rhythmically rising
to meet the stone harbor wall.
Impossibly large luxury launches,
once glistening white in sparkling blue,
were now looming shadows.
Fog had swallowed them and their owners,
swallowed too their brittle white smiles,
leaving only clink of their crystal
and the rank stench of their privilege.

Into my mind came sun and heat,
the vulnerable chug and cough
of an ancient diesel motor
powering an overcrowded, flimsy boat
filled with desperation, hope and fear.
I felt again the salt-laden clothes,
saw the gathering sea, the looming swell,
heard the creaking of the water-filling vessel.

Then another vision came,
one that I could not shake,
the streets of the city aflame,
angry mobs rampaging,
tear gas clouds, baton charges,
the vulnerable trampled,
dark stains flowing through blood-filled squares.
I groped blindly then stumbled.
I stared into the blankness.
In the distance, dim, shrouded,
a light still faintly shone.
I stretched my arm out to it.

Could I grasp it or would the fog,
rolling in ever more thickly,
extinguish it altogether?

Dispersion

Many voices rise in futile protest
as the bloated king sits in self-admiration
in his mirror-filled room,
plotting, scheming, bellowing out boasts,
a nightmare combination of rat-cunning and vanity,
while fog, carrying poisonous toxicity,
makes an insidious way through the entire city.

It winds past the manicured lawns
of the who-gives-a-shit grifters.
It disperses into potholed suburbs
where deserted factories with broken windows
cry out against abandonment.
It whispers promises of restored privilege.
It sings of entitlement and revenge.
It celebrates division, greed and hate.

Is there a cleansing wind?
Will, on one fine day, a fair breeze
blow the fog away
or will lingering toxicity
render my much loved city
into the likeness of a bed-ridden patient
whose vitality has evaporated?
Is the period of greatness of this city
I love coming to an end?
Will its sole remaining joy lie
in raising the flag of long gone glory?
Will this deep fog cause each successive day
to fade further into enfeebled diminishment?

Nightmare

Last night I dreamt of a house
with golden doors open wide,
liberty written on its walls
and equality glowing inside.

Then I saw smiling thieves
in tailored suits and ties,
deceitful intent glibly oiled
by well-practiced lies.

They stole the shining treasure,
stripped the jeweled beams,
carried off the golden orbs
that lit the House of Dreams.

They left the merest shadow,
a painted, empty facade,
and everything they spewed out
was stained deceptive fraud.

Then I awoke drenched
from the horror I had seen,
blood oozing through the door
of the ruined House of Dreams.

At the Hustings

You who with me rule, listen:

Shed no tears for the dead or dying.
There is no money in that.

Think not upon the future.
Take your profit now.

Poverty and inequality are always with us.
Your wealth is yours alone.

Come.
I set you free.
Accept liberty.
Insularity
is security,
honesty
a mere commodity.
Gather to yourself
beautiful wealth.

Go forth.

Exploit, exploit, exploit.

On Massacres in Schools

The king rose early,
saddled his donkeys and took
his subject children up the mountain.

The children said
Where is the offering, our father,
and who is this god we praise?

You are the offering, my children.

Then hail of fire descended
and bright blood flowed until all were gone.
The king sighed, thought he would pray
as he descended the mountain.

A cry of grief rose from the city,
but still a large crowd gathered
to welcome and praise the king.

It's hard, the king said,
so hard but what can we do?
We don't wish it but we must worship.

Then the great crowd shouted

Amen.

On War

Fog clouds the violence coursing
through the arteries of the empire.
Fog clouds its flowering,
the dark lumps lodging in tangle of wire,
muddy trenches, gas, acres of green grass,
neat white crosses, bleak eyes staring
behind razor wire or skeletons
uncovered from shallow pits.

Fog clouds the young men
carrying home dark cells.
It hides the metastasizing,
the waking at night,
the hissing of pills and booze
that flames in white rage and scorches
all who stand too close,
shrinking wife, sobbing daughter,
son trapped between anger and love.

Fog clouds the corporations
growing swollen and fat
from feeding on violence.
Fog hides how war is sold
to the young and gullible.
Fog wraps it in a flag,
or the promise of greatness,
or the gross deceit
that the necessary cure exists
in multiplying the tumors.
Fog muffles the women weeping
for the folly of the world
but it cannot hide the waste,

the terrible, terrible waste
rising high above the fog
into the water shedding sky.

On Huck Finn

—for Joan Colby

A friend once wrote
that Tom married Becky,
became a lawyer, then a judge,
forgot his vibrant youth,
harrumphed and carved the roast
and settled into opinionated age.

That's not true for you, Huck,
weeping over the dark heart of your fellows,
triumphing in goodness over faulty conscience.

They say you lit out for the Territory
but you have had many guises.
I know you re-appeared in Greenwich Village
in the 1960's with curly long hair,
dreamy eyes and a bag full of songs
about the folly and darkness
of the mighty river of your country.

We need you on your raft again,
writing and singing of all you see.
The King and the Duke are still with us,
lying, cheating, vilely manipulating.
The Shepherdsons and Grangerfords still feud
and the murderous madness of the mob threatens.

Come again, Huck. Re-appear.
We need your truthfulness and your vision.
That at least is a kind of liberty.

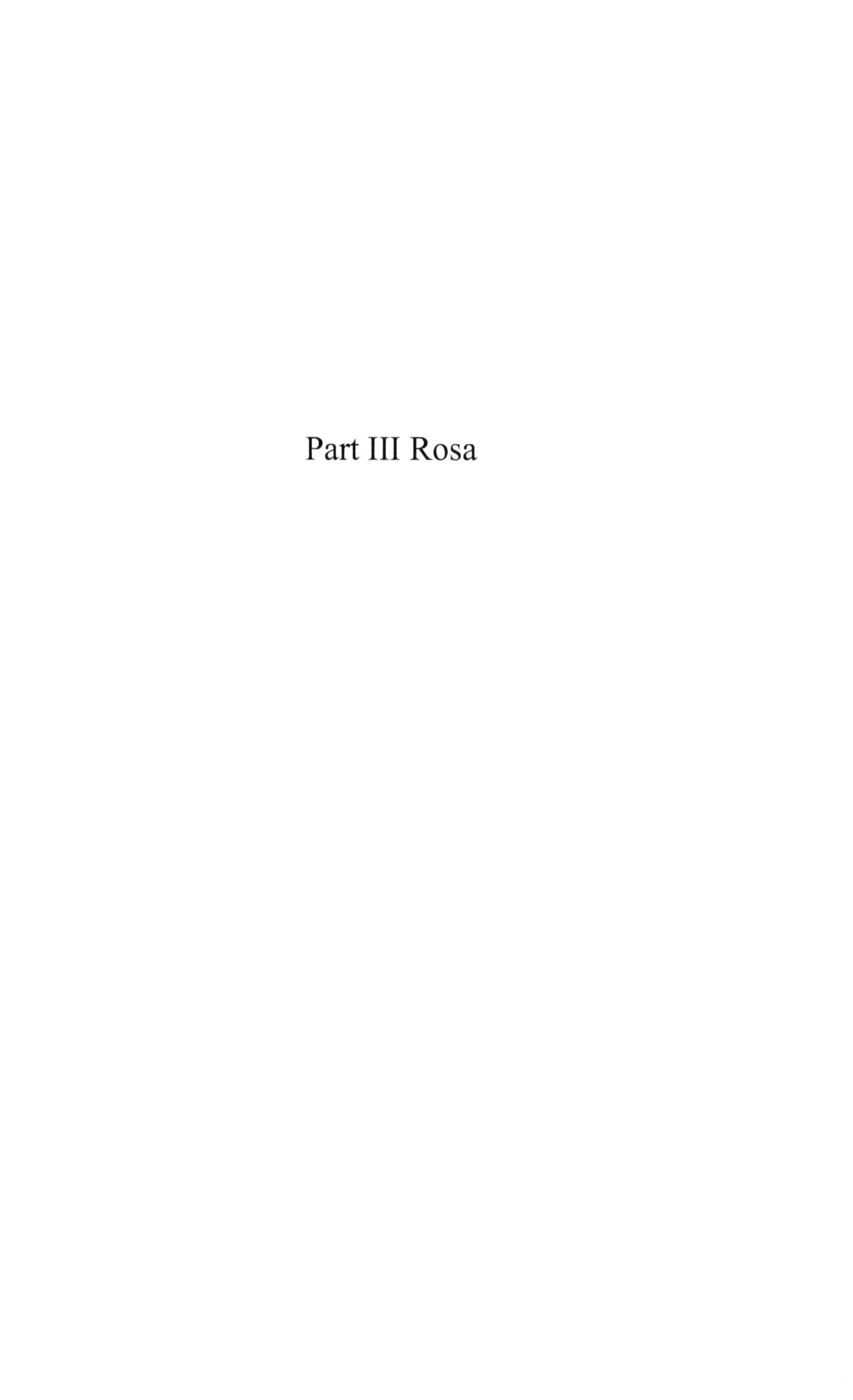

Part III Rosa

see, Morteza,
how fog decorates
the spider's silken geometry
with diamond drops of dew

remember, Morteza,
the deepest descending dark
most brilliantly displays
night’s blaze of cosmic light

love, Morteza,
is the butterfly wing
we dry in the dappled dawning

love, Morteza,
is light's brightness
rising above thick grey fog

love, Morteza,
is the cord that entwines
your pulsing heart to mine

love, Morteza,
is our guiding star
leading us through fog and night

Gift

Sometimes darkness dominates.
Young men step on mines.
Young women visit markets
where, lying in stealth,
are bombs and lost limbs
and a future robbed of hope.
Shunned, crippled, abandoned,
robbed of hope, they dare not dream
but you have healing in your hands.
Your gift dances through rooms
once shuttered and dark.
Then curtains billow.
and from grey days spring
fresh petals of brightness.
Songs of tomorrow sound again.
You bring the blue of day.
You cannot fix everything but you can
sweep some darkness away.

A Beam of Light

We are only our dreams
so why shouldn't we,
with prophets and seers,
float out of our darkened window
on a beam of pure light,
soaring high above the fog,
floating beyond swamp and desert
to see, just over the horizon,
a new world rising out of the dark,
that one where justice descends
like the morning dew,
swords are beaten into ploughshares
and peace, like a mantle,
covers the glistening earth.

Rosa’s Choice

We have heard the orphan’s cry
and the widow’s groan.
We have seen the limbless victims of war.
We take what gifts we can
to both suffering and joy,
your healing hands,
our touch, soft and gentle as a kiss,
our words, kind like healing balm
and empathy that is palm to palm.

We wake

to the flickering screen's
images of desperation and remorse,
the bleak recounting
of misdeeds, lies, greed, corruption,
scenes of anger, partisan politics, accusation,
analysis, implication, expectation, speculation,

but above the fog
is a blue-sky day,
gum trees in nectar-filled
explosion of blossom,
air filled with flocks
of beautiful rainbow lorikeets
descending to joyously feast
with their excited chatter
and grey friar birds,
dipping their dark heads
to fill their curved beaks,
singing their strange
chokk-chokk-four-o-clock
in unrestrained, joyous, raucous celebration.

The Forge

The golden bird on golden bough
first came from furnace fire,
dross removed, skillfully hammered
into object of desire.

The curving razor sword that glints
along its lustrous length
was heated, folded, beaten
into its shining strength.

We much desire the forged-steel strength
but not the hammer blows,
yet we must bend before the forge
from which the luster grows.

Beyond the fog

are myriad stars,
diamond points of night
embroidering the midnight sky.
On days dark and cloudy
spoked columns of light
descend like ladders from high.
Behind the zephyr waft
is a vast, relentless, shifting heft.
Within the shimmer of the sea
is the crash on cliff and cleft.
Rivers flow from source to sea
in endless circularity
and wind and water inevitably turn
walls and towers into dust.

Come

It is the dawn. We must return.
Spring's blue freshness is in the air.
The bitterness of fog is leaving.
A day arises that is calm and fair.

Think not on what lies behind or ahead.
Press on in courage and belief.
Each day's journey is sufficient to itself.
Each day will contain joy and grief.

Night is coming when travel ceases.
Winter will bring bitter states
but beyond the night and winter's chill
our calling, our purpose, waits.

As long as you travel by my side
of each day's trials what do I care?
Even the burdens in the blue-black clouds
in hindsight can seem as light as air.

So, let us be gone. Let us travel together
through jubilation and sorrow.
Hand in hand we support each other.
Resolutely we face tomorrow.

Part IV Atefeh

A Day Like Any Other

It was a day like any other.
The sun was hot, the sky cloudless.
I walked to the market.
I love the noise and color,
stalls filled with bright red pomegranates,
grapes green and black,
figs and dates plump and delicious,
nuts, dried beans and spices,
the beautiful aroma of fresh bread.
I was sixteen, young, healthy,
filled with dreams and ambition.
Then a great hot blast lifted me off the ground.
My ears felt like they would burst.
The world was falling.
Buildings were crumbling.
There was smoke and dust,
acrid stench, screams and moans.
I was being picked up and carried.
The pain in my legs was terrible.
Then everything went dark.

I awoke in hospital.
I was one of the lucky ones.
That day nearly one hundred died.
Many, many more were injured,
lots of them worse than me.
My legs were gone
but I was not burnt or disfigured.
Do not weep.
Here we must accept suffering.
I am not alone.

My country is full of limbless ones.
That is why you return each year.
You know that I am poor
and my family can never pay
for the expensive limbs you bring.
You want to know why you should help me.

This.

If you give me these legs
I will continue my education
and I will help others.
I will grasp the second chance like a rebirth.
Our poor cry out for learning.
Girls are imprisoned by poverty and ignorance.
Children are neglected or abandoned.
My work will be to help them.
Then you will have helped all those that I touch.
I will make both of our lives deep praise.
You will be my silent partner.
Together we will help multitudes.
This is the promise I make to you this day.

God's Will

People say that it is God's Will
that the bomb exploded and took my legs.
They say that I must accept that Will.

Then I say to them:

God did not make those explosives.
God did not pack them in a truck.
God did not drive it to a crowded market.
God did not strew the street with blood and limbs.
God did not take my legs.
God did not make widows, widowers, orphans.
God did not leave parents bereft and grieving.
I say people have done these things.
I say their words are an excuse to justify horror.
I say to them that until we accept responsibility
everything stays as it is.
I say that this is our world
and we must work so that children
no longer sit hungry and abandoned,
the poor no longer cry out for mercy
and that people visiting a market
no longer have the fear
of being robbed of life or hope.
I say to them that God has given us
the power and freedom to choose.
I say to them that God must weep
when He looks at our world.
I say to them that I will work
for good, for love, for change.

I say that is God’s Will.
I say that I will never lie down behind their lie.
How do they respond?
They shuffle a little, cough, clear their throat,
say it is late and they must leave.
I am not so foolish as to think
that I have changed their minds
but I must act and I will, even without legs.
But doctor, I will think
that acts of goodness are godly
and perhaps it is the Will of God
that you have come here to help me.

Freedom

We had no freedom.
Our leader was a cruel man.
He had the power to do as he pleased
and it pleased him to do many bad things.
I know clever people like you
had to flee for your lives.
I know you found safety and wealth elsewhere
and some of you may be honest
in your desire to bring freedom to us.
But our country lies in ruin.
Our cities are rubble.
The treasures of our past are stolen.
Neighbor rises against neighbor.
Destruction and death are everywhere.
Your people have done this.
The dream of freedom is wonderful
but what use is that freedom
when we cannot walk the streets in safety?

River

This ancient river we gaze upon,
older than civilization,
older than empire and kings and war,
flows past banks, where long ago
great walled cities flourished.
Proud kings strutted and boasted
of their wealth and their power.
High walls glazed with blue,
wide enough for chariots,
gave the illusion of safety.
Young men, armed with sword, spear and bow,
marched out to conquer distant lands.
They brought back gold, jewels and slaves.
City squares filled with the clamor of commerce,
palaces with the malice of plotting,
evenings with lovers' whispers and pledges.
Where are they now?
They are dust.
Time has buried them
and all their machinations.
Let kings boast.
Let power rise and fall.
In this brief moment of my life
I seek things that last.
What is there but doing good,
loving mercy and believing
that love can triumph and reign
in this small heart of mine.

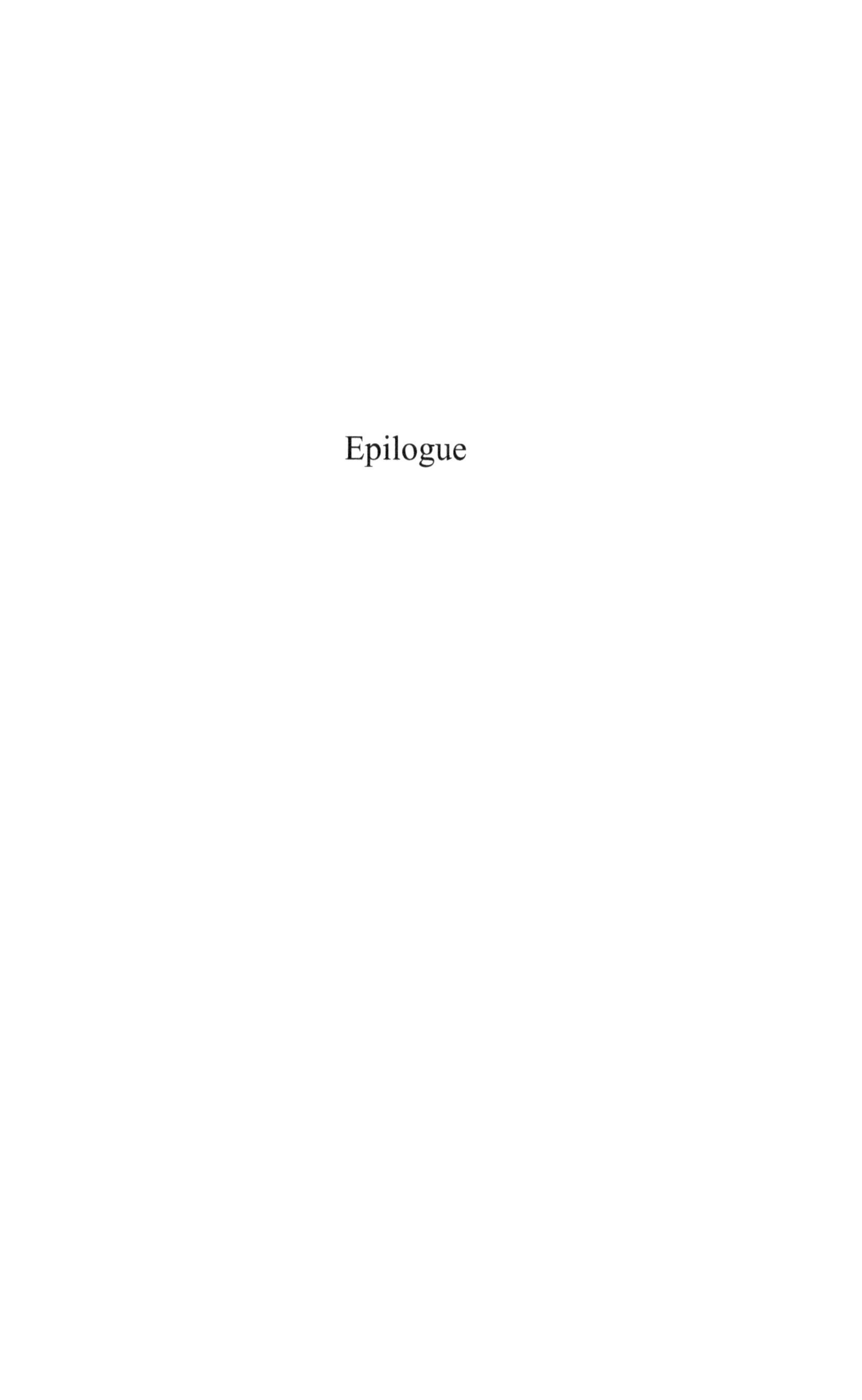

Epilogue

Praise

I am not afraid.
You have come back
as I knew you would.
Your hand, like your eyes,
is soft and kind.
The wardsman pushes me
and you walk beside me.
Hate stole my limbs
and robbed me of hope.
Now this door opens.
They smile to see me.
They have come with you from afar.
How is it that I am so lucky?
This one tells me I will sleep
and when I awake
they will teach me to walk again.
It will be dawn.
New life awaits.
I will live well.
I will celebrate kindness.
I will be generous.
I will bless you.
I will be praise.
I stretch out my arm.
There is the needle.
Count to ten, she says.
I count.
I sleep.
I sleep.

I

sleep….

About the Author

Neil Creighton is an Australian poet whose work as a teacher of English and Drama brings him into close contact with thousands of young lives, most happy and triumphant but too many tragically filled with neglect or poverty. It makes him intensely aware of how opportunity is so unequally proportioned and his work often reflects a strong interest in social justice. He has been widely published, both online and in hard copy in places such as “Poets Reading the News”, “Peacock Journal”, “Autumn Sky Daily” “New Verse News”, “Prosopisia” and “The Second Genesis”. His published works are “Earth Music” (Praxis), “Loving Leah” (Kelsay), “Awakening” (Cyberwit) and “Rock Dreaming” (Kelsay). He is a Contributing Editor at “Verse-Virtual”, an online poetry journal.

www.ingramcontent.com/pod-product-compliance
Lightning Source LLC
LaVergne TN
LVHW010543100826
845148LV00013B/2579
9781639800742